BIBLE VISUALS international

Helping Children See Jesus

ISBN: 978-1-64104-073-0

Bible Lessons for Life's Journey

Author: Katherine E. Hershey
Illustrator: Frances E. Hertzlerr Front Cover: Linda McInturff
Typesetting and Layout: Morgan Melton, Patricia Pope

© 2018 Bible Visuals International
PO Box 153, Akron, PA 17501-0153
Phone: (717) 859-1131
www.biblevisuals.org

RELATED ITEMS

To access related items (such as activities, memory verse posters and translated texts) please visit our web store at shop.biblevisuals.org and enter 5040 in the search box on the page.

FREE TEXT DOWNLOAD

To access a FREE printable copy of the teaching text (PDF format) in English or other available languages, enter S5040DL in the search box. Add the item to your cart, and use coupon code XTACSV17 at checkout. Once your order is processed you will receive an email with a link to the free download.

Acts 16:31

Believe on the Lord Jesus Christ and thou shalt be saved, and thy house.

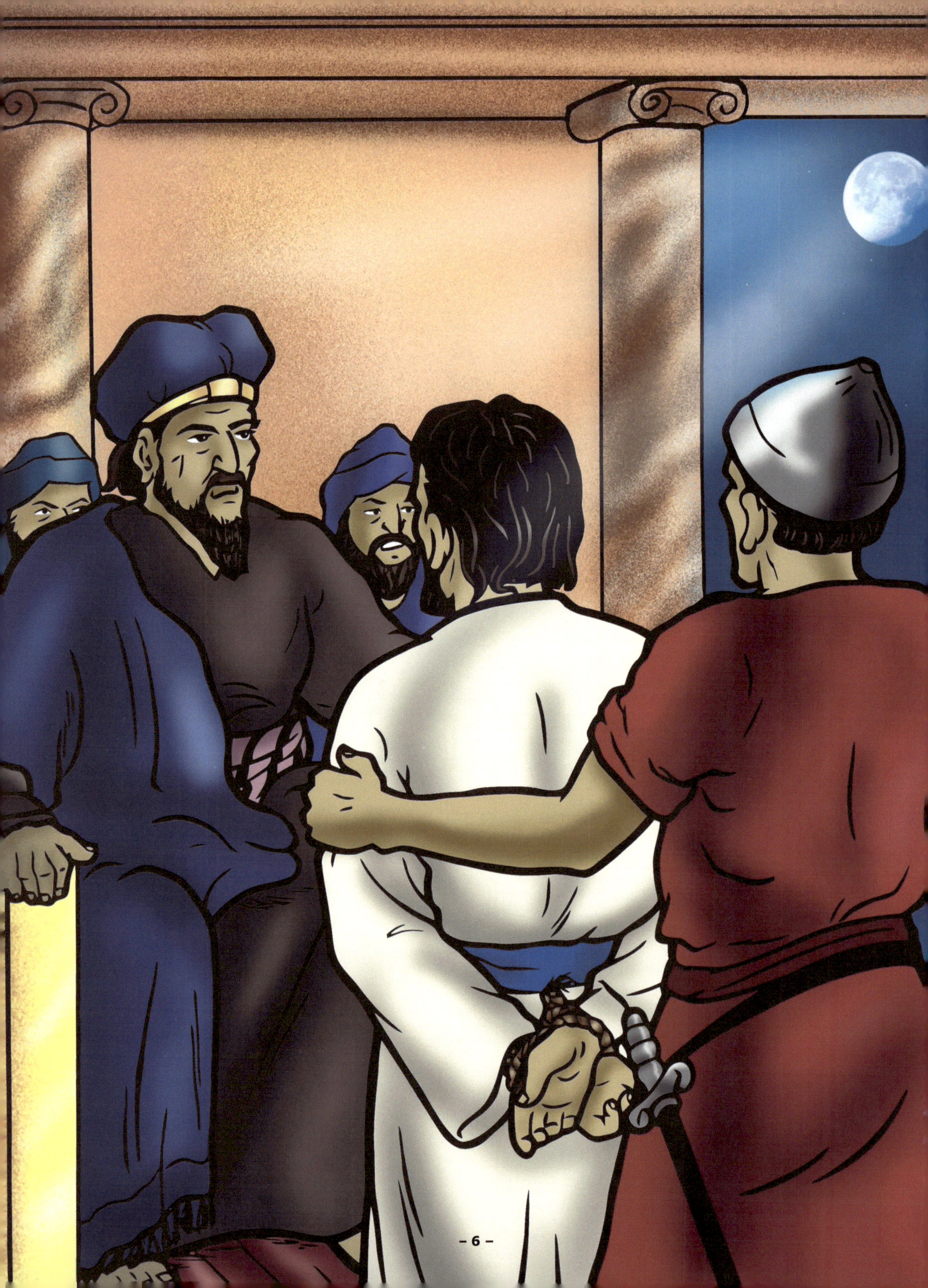

Isaiah 53:6

All we like sheep have gone astray, we have turned every one to his own way; and the Lord hath laid on Him the iniquity of us all.

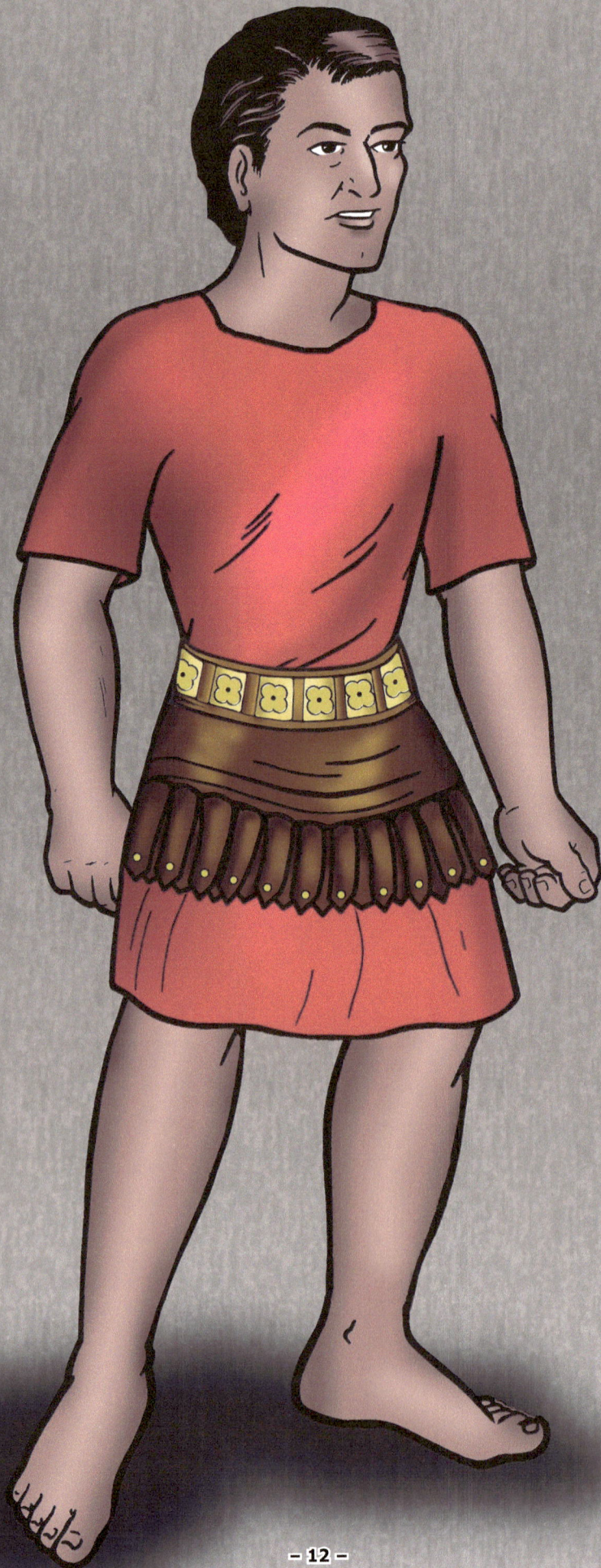

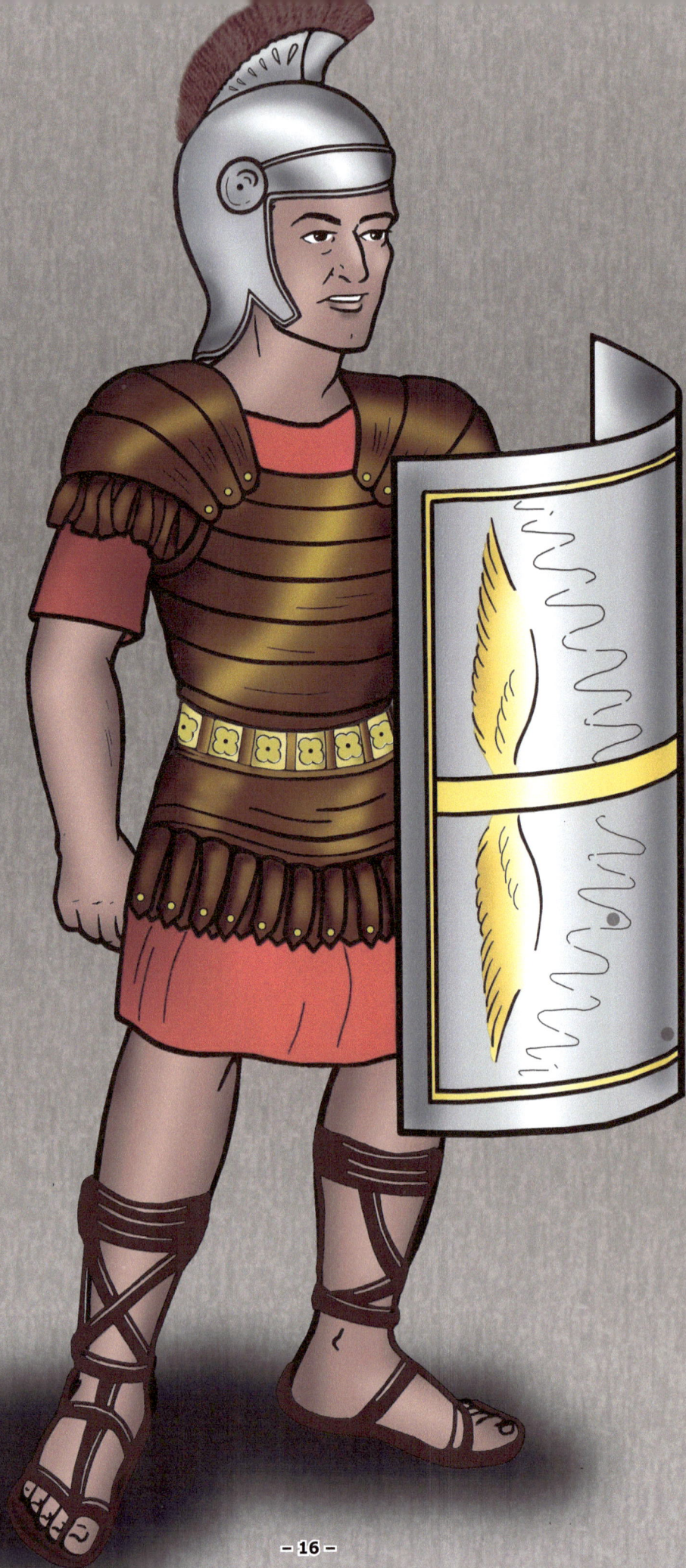

Ephesians 6:11

Put on the whole armor of God, that ye may be able to stand against the wiles of the devil.

Jeremiah 33:3

Call unto Me, and I will answer thee, and show thee great and mighty things, which thou knowest not.

John 3:18

He that believeth on Him is not condemned: but he that believeth not is condemned already, because he hath not believed in the Name of the only begotten Son of God.

Scripture to be studied: Acts 16:16-34

Memory Verse:

Believe on the Lord Jesus Christ and thou shalt be saved. (Acts 16:31)

Aim of the Lesson: To answer two questions:

1. How can I get rid of my burden of sin?
2. What must I do to be saved? (To show students their need and the One Who can meet that need.)

The missionary party was following its marching orders given by God. It was Paul who had received the orders one night as he slept. As he dreamed, a man from the land of Macedonia appeared to him and said, "Come over into Macedonia, and help us."

Paul told Silas and the others about it. "I know it was more than a dream. I know it was a message from the Lord. We must change our plans and go to Macedonia." Everyone agreed that it was a message from God. The men were ready and eager to carry to a new land the good news about the Lord Jesus Christ, the Son of God.

Show Illustration # 1

Those were busy days of preaching the Gospel in a new city. They were exciting days, too–and difficult ones! "The biggest problem in our work seems to be that girl," Paul decided. And the other missionaries agreed with him.

"Of course we know she isn't right in her mind. Those wicked men have her in their power. They've made people believe that she can tell fortunes. They're making a lot of money."

Every day the girl followed them through the streets of the city. She shouted at the top of her voice, "These men are the servants of the Most High God! They show us the way of salvation!" Over and over she repeated it. What she said was really true! But because everyone knew that she did not have her right mind, people had nothing to do with the missionaries. As Paul and the other missionaries went to the place where they gathered to pray, they talked to God about it. "Heavenly Father, we've come to this country because we are following Your directions. Help us to know what to do about this girl. Give us the opportunity to show someone how to be saved." Paul knew God loved the girl, as well as the rest of the people in the city. God loves you, too, no matter who you are.

Again the girl followed them down the street. "These men are the servants of the Most High God! They show us the way of salvation!" she screamed. Suddenly Paul knew exactly what to do. He knew that it was the power of Satan which made the girl act as she did.

So he turned around and cried to the wicked spirit, "I command you in the Name of Jesus Christ to come out of her." Immediately the girl was well! She was in her right mind!

Show Illustration #2

The men in the crowd began shouting angrily. Rushing to missionaries Paul and Silas, they yelled angry threats. "What are you doing in our city? You're only bringing trouble!"

Paul and Silas knew that these were the men who kept that poor girl in their power. They were angry because they couldn't use her to tell fortunes anymore. Before anyone had opportunity to explain, the men grabbed Paul and Silas and dragged them (probably by the feet, cf. Acts 14:19) through the streets of the city. The crowd followed. At the marketplace the men took Paul and Silas before the city police chiefs. "These men do not belong in our city!" they screamed. "They are strangers here. They are bringing a great deal of trouble to our city. They are teaching things which are not for us. They do not belong here. Get rid of them!"

"They will be punished," the city officials answered. "Take off their clothes!" Their clothes were ripped off. "Beat them!" the police commanded. Long whips were used. The whips lashed across their bare backs until Paul and Silas were bruised and cut and bleeding.

Paul and Silas remembered how the Lord Jesus suffered for them. He, too, was beaten and bruised. The Bible says the Lord Jesus suffered for sins that He might bring us to God. (See 1 Peter 3:18.) He did not suffer for His sins, because He had none. He is the perfect Son of God. He suffered for your sins and mine. God must punish sin. And Christ Jesus took the punishment we deserve when He suffered and died.

"Throw them into jail!" the police demanded. As they were turned over to the jailor, the city officials gave him their last command: "Be sure to keep them safely. Don't let them escape!" The jailor obeyed that order.

Show Illustration #3

Paul and Silas were put in the dungeon of the prison. There was no window. The walls and floor were cold and damp.

Their feet were fastened in stocks. Their backs were cut and bleeding. They were stiff and sore. They could not lie down. They could not stand up. How slowly time passed, one hour after another! Even though the dungeon was cold, the air was stale.

"Let's pray," one of them suggested. And pray they did. What do you think they prayed about? (Discuss, leading to thought of praising God, too.) Praying helped a great deal to take their minds off their miserable surroundings. Then, as they finished praying, it seemed right that they should sing. They sang and sang and sang. And almost before they realized it, it was midnight. But Paul and Silas were still singing praises to God in that cold, dreary, smelly dungeon. No sound like that had ever been heard in the dungeon. Cursing and screaming–yes! But praying and singing–never!

Suddenly there was an earthquake. The prison walls shook! Stones fell. The chains came out of the wall. Doors flew off their hinges. And the stocks opened. Paul and Silas were free! The other prisoners were all free! But no one ran away. They were too surprised and afraid.

The jailor ran in. If any of those prisoners escaped, he would be punished by death!

He saw the open doors, the broken chains, the freed prisoners! Then he grabbed his sword. He pointed it toward his heart. He would rather kill himself than to have his life taken by the city officials.

"Stop!" Paul shouted. "Don't hurt yourself. We are all here!"

Show Illustration #4

"Get me a light!" shouted the jailor. When he could see, he looked all around. Not one prisoner had escaped. Shaking from fear, the jailor fell on his knees before Paul and Silas. "Sirs, what must I do to be saved?" he cried.

"Believe on the Lord Jesus Christ and thou shalt be saved and thy house " (Acts 16:31).

That jailor did believe! He believed that he was a sinner. He believed that the Lord Jesus died on the cross for his sins. He believed that He rose from the dead. He believed that He would give everlasting life to him if he would invite Him to come into his heart and life. Immediately he invited Him to come in.

Paul and Silas were taken out of that awful dungeon to the jailor's own house. All of his family came together to hear the story of what had happened. They heard, too, how the jailor "believed on the Lord Jesus Christ." And each member of his family also believed on Him and received Him.

The jailor then took warm water and a soft cloth, and ever so gently washed the sore backs of the missionaries. His wife fixed a delicious meal for them. Never before had food tasted so good! It was a never-to-be-forgotten night for Paul and Silas–and for the jailor, too.

The joy in the hearts of the missionaries overflowed. They were happy to be free. But they were even happier because there were those in that new land who had believed on the Lord Jesus Christ and were saved.

Invitation

Did you hear how that jailor was saved from his sins and how he received everlasting life? *He* knew he was a sinner. *He* knew it because of the wrong things he had done in his life. (Maybe right now *you* are thinking about the wrong things *you* have done.) Then he believed that the Lord Jesus died on the cross for his sins. He believed, too, that the Lord Jesus rose from the dead. (Do you believe this?) Listen carefully! He believed that the Lord Jesus would give him everlasting life if he would invite Him to come into his life.

If you believe these truths about the Lord Jesus, if you want your sins forgiven, ask Him to come into your life right now as we bow our heads and pray.

Lesson 2

THE CRUCIFIXION AND RESURRECTION

Scripture to be Studied: Matthew 26-28; Mark 14-16; Luke 22-24; John 18-20

Memory Verse:

All we like sheep have gone astray; we have turned everyone to his own way, and the Lord hath laid on Him the iniquity of us all. (Isaiah 53:6)

Aim of the Lesson: To show that men and women and children are lost sheep for whom the Good Shepherd gave His life. Because our sin was laid on Him, we can be free from the burden of sin.

The disciples of the Lord Jesus did not always understand all that He said. One day He was speaking about the sheep and the shepherd. Then He explained, "I am the good Shepherd. The good Shepherd gives His life for the sheep."

Of course, the disciples knew that God had often spoken of people as sheep. (We saw that in our memory verse, didn't we?) The disciples knew the Old Testament Scriptures. So they were not surprised when God the Son spoke of people as "sheep." They could even understand when the Lord Jesus spoke of Himself as the Shepherd.

A shepherd took his flock to places where the grass was nice and green. He led the sheep to clear, fresh water. He protected the sheep from danger. At night he led them safely to the fold. The disciples knew the Psalm which begins, "The Lord is my Shepherd."

No, it was not hard for them to understand that the Lord Jesus would take care of His people. And surely He would be the good Shepherd. But what did He mean about "giving His life"? This was the part they could not understand.

The wonderful life He lived proved to the disciples that the Lord Jesus was the very Son of God. That is why they could not understand when He talked about dying. Surely, since He was the Son Whom God had promised to send, He would not die, would He?

One night the Lord Jesus had a special supper with His disciples. Once more He tried to make them understand that He would soon die. But again, they could not understand what He said. Later that night Peter and James and John went with Him to a garden to pray.

Suddenly the quiet of the dark night was shattered. Men shouted. Torches blazed. Angry men and soldiers rushed toward the Lord Jesus. Peter, James and John saw it all. The mob grabbed the Lord Jesus. The disciples scattered everywhere, like frightened sheep. Only John was near the Saviour. Peter followed the crowd, far, far away from the Son of God.

The Lord Jesus was pushed by the mob. Where were they taking Him at this hour of the night? It was after midnight.

Show Illustration #5

Finally they shoved Him to the house of the high priest. The high priest was not in bed as you might think. He was expecting them to come! He wanted to see the Lord Jesus put to death. It was up to him to find some reason why the Son of God should be killed. While the Saviour stood in front of him, some wicked men were brought in. They told lies about God's Son. But none of the men agreed. Each liar made the others sound untrue. Through it all the Lord Jesus kept absolutely silent.

Finally the high priest demanded, "Tell us! Are you the Christ, the Messiah, the Promised One of God?"

The precious Lord Jesus looked right into the eyes of the high priest and answered, "I am!"

The crowd shouted. "It's not true! He lies! It's blasphemy. He's pretending to be God's Promised One. But He's not!" They refused to believe that the Lord Jesus did tell the truth.

They would not believe that He is the One whom God had sent. Some men slapped Him. They spit in His face. "Now we have a reason for putting Him to death," they howled. "He says He's the Son of God. We know He's not."

Then they led Him away from the high priest's house and took Him to Pilate, the governor of the country. It was early in the morning. Pilate did not want to be bothered at such an hour. "What has He done? Why don't you judge Him by your own law?" Pilate demanded.

They shouted, "Our law doesn't permit us to crucify a man. We want this Man to die by crucifixion."

Pilate took special notice then. He had not realized that this Man was wicked enough to deserve the death sentence! "What evil has He done?" Pilate asked. "I can't sentence a man to death without knowing why he should die."

"He says He's the King of the Jews!" they shouted.

"Are You a king?" Pilate demanded.

"I am," the Lord Jesus replied. "But my kingdom is not of this world. It is from Heaven." Pilate did not understand Him.

"I can find no fault in Him," Pilate said. "I will have Him whipped and set Him free." They brought out the whips–terrible things, with tiny bits of glass and stone fastened in the leather. They cut deeply with each lash of the whip into the back of the precious Son of God. Then Pilate's soldiers made a crown from a thornbush. They dressed Him in a purple robe. (Purple was the color worn by kings.) This was their way of making fun of Him. They put a stick in His hand. They knelt before Him, laughing. "Hail, King of the Jews!" they shouted.

Pilate took Him out before the crowd, hoping that when they saw how He had already suffered, they would be satisfied. But the crowd screamed, "Crucify Him! Crucify Him! By our law He ought to die, because He made Himself the Son of God."

Pilate was afraid. He demanded of the Lord Jesus: "Where are you from? To what country do you belong?" The Lord Jesus did not say one word.

"Don't you know that I have the power to crucify You, or to set You free?" he asked.

"You would have no power at all," answered the Lord Jesus, "if it were not given to you from above."

Pilate was more afraid than ever. Once more he tried to set the Lord Jesus free. But again the crowd roared: "If you set Him free you are not a friend of the king!"

Pilate did not want to lose important friends. He did not want to lose his high office. So he turned the dear Son of God over to the wicked people.

"You take Him," he commanded. Those evil men did take Him. They led Him up a hill, forcing Him to carry His own cross.

Show Illustration #6

On Calvary's hill, those wicked men nailed Him to that cross. They nailed two criminals to crosses–one on each side of Him.

"If you are the Son of God," cried one of the criminals, "save Yourself and us!"

"Aren't you afraid to talk that way?" the other thief demanded. "We deserve to die for the crimes we've committed. But this Man has done nothing wrong."

Then he looked at the Lord Jesus. "Lord, remember me when You come in Your kingly glory," he prayed. That thief believed that the Lord Jesus was the Christ, the Son of God. He had not done anything wrong. He was the only One who would come again in kingly glory!

How wonderful for the Lord Jesus to have heard those words–words of love, when all around was hate! What peace and joy came to the heart of the dying thief when he heard the Lord Jesus say, "Truly, I tell you, today you shall be with Me in Paradise." The sin of that criminal's heart was forgiven! He was forgiven because the Son of God was dying for Him.

Even at the last minute His friends were certain that the Lord Jesus would do something to save Himself.

"If you are the Son of God," the unbelieving crowd shouted, "come down from the cross, and we will believe."

But He did not come down. He could have, had He chosen to do so. The nails were not what held Him to that cross. The love that He had for the world, the love that the heavenly Father had for the world, the love He has for you–this is what kept Him on the cross.

"All we like sheep have gone astray; we have turned every one to his own way; and the LORD [God] hath laid on Him [the Lord Jesus] the iniquity of us all" (Isaiah 53:6).

Worse than all the awful pain of crucifixion was the pain of having our sin laid on Him. Having our sin laid on Him meant that He was being blamed for everyone's sin–all the wrong that would be done by men and women and boys and girls to the very end of time–all that sin was put on Him. The perfect, sinless Son of God took. not only the blame for every person's sin, He took the punishment for it. The good Shepherd was giving His life for the straying sheep. If the Lord Jesus had come down from that cross, there would have been no salvation. No one could ever have gone to Heaven. It was His love–love for you and for me–that held Him there for six awful hours.

Show Illustration #7

Later, loving hands took His dead body off the cross. Very tenderly they wrapped it in grave clothes and laid it in a newly made tomb. A huge stone sealed the tomb. And guards stood watch so that no one could steal His body.

Then each one hurried to his home to observe the Sabbath day. That was a day of rest. This particular Sabbath day was a day of darkness–the darkest day in all the world–for those who had known and loved the Son of God. He was dead. Many who had believed in Him wondered if they had been wrong. The disciples gathered together in a secret hiding place. As they talked about the things which had happened, it seemed like a horrible dream. And yet they knew it was true. The Lord Jesus was dead. They could not understand it.

Show Illustration #8

Very early in the morning on the first day of the week, some women rushed to the disciples with a strange story. "We went to the tomb to take spices to put on the body of the Lord Jesus. When we reached the tomb we saw that the stone was rolled away from the door. Angels in shining garments were there. They asked, 'Why do you look for the living among the dead? Jesus is not here. He is risen!'"

They continued, "Can it be true? His body is gone. He's not in the tomb. Do you think He has really risen from the dead?"

The men agreed quickly that this sounded impossible. One commanded, "Peter! John! You go to the tomb. See what has really happened. Then come back and tell us the truth."

Peter and John hurried to the tomb. Surely enough, it was empty. Still the disciples were not convinced. Evening came, and the disciples were all together. They were still afraid. The doors and windows of the room were locked.

Show Illustration #9

And suddenly the Son of God was standing there! Terror filled the disciples' hearts.

Then the Lord Jesus spoke. "Peace to you! Why are you disturbed and troubled? See My hands and My feet. It is I, Myself. This is what I was trying to make you understand," He said. "It was written in the Scriptures that I would have to suffer for the sin of the world."

At last they understood. The good Shepherd had to give His life for the sheep who went astray. But because the good Shepherd is the Son of God He had risen to live forever. And joy filled the hearts of the disciples–joy such as they had never known before.

(*Teacher:* If you are not using the *Pilgrim's Progress* story, you may want to give the following invitation here.)

Invitation

The Lord Jesus gave His life for your sin. And He lives today. He wants to be *your* good Shepherd and live in your heart. He asks that you trust Him and invite Him to come into your heart and life. Will you ask Him now? He will come in! (See Revelation 3:20.)

Lesson 3
THE CHRISTIAN'S ARMOR

NOTE TO THE TEACHER

If you are teaching this lesson along with the story of Pilgrim, you will want to incorporate it in the chapter "Pilgrim's Armor." The lessons will be more interesting if you speak of Pilgrim as you describe each part of the armor.

If you are not teaching *Pilgrim's Progress*, introduce the lesson with the following paragraph:

Do you know that everyone who receives the Lord Jesus as his Saviour also receives a wonderful suit of armor? Every Christian must fight many battles against Satan. God knows that we do not have the strength to win these battles. So He gives us a belt, a breastplate, shoes which never wear out, a shield to hold in one hand, a helmet for our head, and a sword to hold. These are all that we need to protect us from our enemy.

Scripture to be Studied: Ephesians 6:10-18

Memory Verse:

Put on the whole armor of God, that ye may be able to stand against the wiles of the devil. (Ephesians 6:11)

Aim of the Lesson: To show the provision God has made in Christ for the Christian to win the victory over Satan.

The Christian soldier is well equipped. Listen closely, now, and get ready for a real surprise, boys and girls.

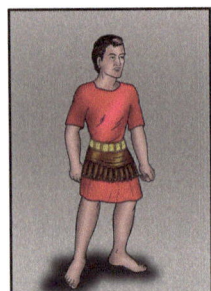

Show Illustration #12

The belt (girdle) is a wide, strong one, and the Bible says that it is a *Belt of Truth*. The belt is to be worn about the loins. (*Teacher:* Webster's definition says: "The part between the lower rib and hipbone." Show students the place where the belt would be worn.) This is the place of strength. When we lift heavy things, we get the strength from the loins. Christians must have protection for their place of strength. What is it that protects their strength? It is the strong belt of *Truth*. An untruthful Christian is the weakest sort of soldier. You can count on it that he will lose every battle. To be a strong Christian, one must be truthful *always*.

Show Illustration #13

The breastplate is that part of the armor which covers the soldier's heart.

And the breastplate which is given to every Christian soldier is the *Breastplate of Righteousness*, or *Right Doing*. Everyone knows that the enemy's target is always the heart. If his arrow or spear hits the soldier's heart, the soldier is finished. So it is most important that the Christian's heart be protected. It is the Christian's heart that causes him to do right (or wrong!) things. And the covering for the heart is the righteousness, or right doing and character of the Lord Jesus, which God Himself gives to those who receive His dear Son.

(We haven't come to the surprise yet!)

Show Illustration #14

The soldier cannot go into the battle barefooted, can he? What kind of shoes do you think the Christian soldier wears?–*Good News of Peace shoes*. The Christian tells others the Good News–the Good News that the Lord Jesus, the Prince of Peace, has come. And no matter how rough the battle, the soldier need not be afraid. God gives him His own peace.

Show Illustration #15

The shield is to protect the soldier from the enemy's arrows or spears. The Christian soldier's shield is the *Shield of Faith*–faith in God's Son. The Lord Jesus has never lost one battle–nor will He ever lose one. No matter how many fiery darts Satan (the wicked prince) sends our way, we have the shield of faith to protect us.

Show Illustration #16

The Christian receives a helmet. What does a helmet protect? The head, of course. That's a pretty important part of the body, is it not? But it has a good protection! Listen! It is the *Helmet of Salvation*. There is no better covering anywhere. One cannot even be a Christian soldier unless he has been saved from his sin. He is saved by coming to the cross, believing that the Lord Jesus died for him there, and receiving Him into his heart. So every Christian has his head (his mind) protected by the helmet of Salvation.

Show Illustration #17

There is something else that the Christian receives. It is a sword. We read in God's Word that the Bible is our sword! It is called the *Sword of the Spirit*. The strong belt, the breastplate, the shoes, the shield, and the helmet protect the soldier from the enemy. But with the sword, the soldier goes after the enemy. It is as we learn God's Word that we can use it as a sword when Satan tempts us.

Now we're ready for the surprise! Do you know that the Christian soldier's armor is not simply some *things*? It is a *Person*! Listen closely.

We have the strong *Belt of Truth*. Who said, "I am the … truth"? It was the Lord Jesus Himself. He who is the Truth keeps us strong by making us truthful. (See John 14:6.)

We have the *Breastplate of Righteousness*, or *Right Doing*. God's Word tells us that the Lord Jesus is Righteousness. (See 1 Corinthians 1:30.) He is the only One who always did right. Because He lives in our hearts, He Himself will protect our hearts.

The *Good News of Peace Shoes* are next. The Bible says that the Lord Jesus is our peace. No wonder we don't have to be afraid in the daily Christian battle. The Prince of Peace is always with us (Ephesians 2:14).

Our *Shield of Faith* is also the Lord Jesus. (See Genesis 15:1.) He who has never lost a battle will stop Satan's fiery darts for He is our shield, our faith. (See Galatians 2:20.)

By now you have guessed that the *Helmet of Salvation* is also the Lord Jesus. He is there always to protect our minds (Psalm 27:1).

While it is true that the *Sword of the Spirit* is the written Word of God, we must tell you that the Lord Jesus is the living Word of God (John 1:1-14). Every day, every moment, no matter where we are, our whole armor is the Lord Jesus Christ Himself. As we give ourselves to Him, we can be certain that He will cause us to win every battle against the wicked prince, Satan.

Invitation

But if you don't have the Lord Jesus you don't have the armor, and you are not in any way protected from Satan's tricks. In fact, you still belong to Satan and cannot count on God's protection. I'm sure that you want this armor of God for your protection. You can have it by receiving the Lord Jesus. If you have not already invited Him to come into your heart, would you like to do so right now, while we pray? If you have received Him before this, thank Him that He lives in your heart.

Lesson 4
THE CROSSING OF THE RED SEA

Scripture to be Studied: Exodus 12:37-51; 14:1-15:2

Memory Verse:

Call unto Me, and I will answer thee, and shew thee great and mighty things, which thou knowest not. (Jeremiah 33:3)

***Aim* of the Lesson:** To show that God will hear our call and use His power to free us from sins that overtake us in our Christian lives.

Of thousands and thousands of Hebrews, not one could remember a time when their people had not been the slaves of a cruel king of Egypt. The king was called Pharaoh. When one Pharaoh died and another came to the throne, the Hebrew people always hoped that the new king would be kind to them. But always it was the same. It seemed that the new Pharaoh was even more cruel than any other Pharaoh had been.

God had given some special promises to His people, the Hebrews. One of the promises was that they would not always live in a land where they would be slaves. God promised that someday they would live in a land of their very own. Finally, after 400 years of slavery, God had set His people free! (See Genesis 15:13; Exodus 12:40.) At last they were on their way to their homeland, the land that God had promised would be their own. In order to guide His people, God used a big cloud. The cloud moved ahead of the men, women and children. It showed them the way to go. At night the cloud turned into a fiery pillar. The fiery pillar gave light to the people as they traveled or camped.

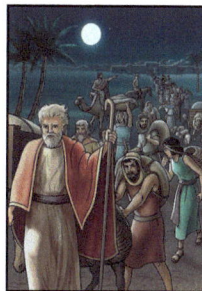

Show Illustration 19

Marching ahead of those thousands of people was Moses. Moses was the man whom God had used to lead His people out of Egypt, away from the cruel king.

The cloud moved, and the people marched. The cloud stopped, and the people camped. While they camped, mothers baked bread for their hungry families. The families enjoyed the bread along with some of the food that they had carried with them out of Egypt. The cloud moved again. The people marched again. Old men and women marched rather slowly. Boys and girls ran ahead of the family groups.

Before long the cloud stopped at the Red Sea. On either side of the crowd were great mountains. In front of them was the sea. What a good place it was to pitch their tents, cook their meals, and rest! How wonderful it was to be able to rest without being afraid that they were going to be punished for resting! The slave drivers in Egypt had never let them rest!

What does it mean to be a slave? (Discuss.) Anything that has great power over *you* can make *you* a slave. You can become a slave to lying. It is possible to lie so much that others never know whether or not you are telling the truth. You can be a slave to fighting. The smallest thing can make you start a fight. You may be a slave to pride–always thinking first of yourself.

Satan makes it easy to sin. Before you know it, you are a slave to some sin. Sin brings punishment. "The wages of sin is death" (Romans 6:23). God's Son, the Lord Jesus Christ, can set you free from sin. He took the punishment for your sin when He died on the cross. If you place all your trust in Him, He will set you free from sin and its wages. Being free from sin is even more wonderful than being free from a cruel king. When the Hebrews were free from the king of Egypt, they had joy—joy which was seen on their faces and heard in their voices.

Show Illustration #20

"I wonder how Pharaoh is going to get his treasure cities built," one of the men said. "Since he doesn't have us to work for him, I doubt if the cities will ever be finished." It was not hard for God's people to remember how the slave drivers had stood over them day after day, forcing them to make bricks for the building.

"I've been thinking about that rich Egyptian family that I worked for," one girl said. "I wonder who is getting their meals, and washing their dishes, and scrubbing their floors." Some of the boys were thinking about the horses and cows of the people for whom they had worked. Who would keep those horses fed? Who would groom them? Who would milk the cows? Everyone agreed that the Egyptians had a lot to learn, now that their slaves were gone.

The people were right. Things were in a mess back in Egypt. Pharaoh was really having his troubles. The men in charge of building the treasure cities had rushed to Pharaoh. "How do you expect us to get cities built? You surely don't think that we're going to make those bricks, do you? We won't make bricks!"

Others of the people of Egypt were demanding an entrance into the royal palace. "Why did you let the Hebrews go?" was the question that everybody asked.

Pharaoh was upset. "All right. All right. We'll bring them back! Get the army together. Get the six hundred best chariots. Get a captain for each. Get all the other chariots of the land. I'll lead the army in my own chariot. It won't take long for our army to catch up with them." Soon the army was on its way. What a cloud of dust those horses and chariots made as they roared over the dry ground! What a noise there was of rumbling chariot wheels, galloping horses' hooves and shouting soldiers!

It might have been the dust cloud that the Hebrew people noticed first. "Does that look like a cloud of dust way over there in the distance?" one man asked.

"I don't know what it is, but it seems to be getting larger. Listen! Do you hear that noise? What is it?" Suddenly the people of God were trembling from head to toe. The color drained from their faces.

"It's Pharaoh's army! They're coming after us to take us back." Quick as a flash everyone in that great crowd knew that Pharaoh was coming. They realized how angry he would be. If he took them back to Egypt, life would be harder than ever before. Perhaps Pharaoh would even kill them here by the sea. They looked around for a way of escape. But there was none.

The high mountains towered on each side of them. The sea was before them. Pharaoh's army was behind them. They were hopelessly trapped!

"Moses!" they yelled to their leader. "Why did you bring us out here to die in the wilderness?"

"Don't be afraid," Moses commanded. "Stand still and see the salvation of the Lord which He will work for you today. You will never see these Egyptians after today. The Lord will

fight for you. You have only to be still and watch." (The words of our memory verse had not yet been written in the Scripture. But Moses knew the truth of them just the same.) And Moses called on God.

Then God spoke to Moses. "Why do you cry to Me? Tell the people to go forward." Forward? The sea was "forward." They could not go that way! But God was not finished with His instructions. "Moses, lift up your rod. Stretch out your hand over the sea."

Show Illustration #21

Moses obeyed. A strong east wind blew. The eyes of the people opened wide. The wind was blowing a path right through the middle of the seal The path became wider and wider. The water piled higher and higher. And the wet, muddy ground became dry.

"Go forward!" Moses shouted. And the hundreds of thousands of people began marching across the wide road right between the water! It was night. The fiery pillar moved to the back of the marching crowd. It gave light to them as they crossed the sea. It stood between the Hebrews and the Egyptian Army. But the same cloud of light that shone for God's people was a wall of darkness to the Egyptians. They could not see what was happening on the other side of that cloud. They could not follow after the Hebrews.

On and on the people marched. Hour after hour through the night they marched. As morning began to dawn and the last person was across the sea, the cloud lifted from behind the marching people and moved in front of them.

Immediately the Egyptians saw what was happening. "After them!" Pharaoh shouted. "Go after them!" The Egyptians plunged between the walls of water. The thundering hooves of the horses and the clatter of the chariots almost drowned out the shouting soldiers. They would recapture those slaves!

The last Egyptian rushed into the path through the sea. Suddenly the path was no longer dry! The chariot wheels were clogged with mud. Someone screamed, "Turn back! Turn back! The God of the Hebrews is fighting for them!"

Show Illustration #22

Then God spoke to Moses again. "Lift up your rod, Moses. Stretch out your hand over the sea." Moses lifted his hand high. Then, crash!

The water fell. The Egyptian army disappeared under the thundering waters of the Red Sea!

How full of awe were God's people! Their hearts bubbled into a glorious song of praise. God had proved His faithfulness. God had kept His promise. He had cared for His own.

Invitation

God's people have a worse enemy than the cruel Pharaoh. You know who he is, do you not? It is Satan. Satan wants to keep you for himself, just as Pharaoh wanted to keep those people as his slaves. (Remember from our story of Pilgrim, that he tried to keep Pilgrim from the cross?) But the Lord Jesus died to set you free. Shall we bow our heads and close our eyes? Now, will you tell God that you do not want to be Satan's slave? Tell Him that right now you are opening your heart and life to the Lord Jesus. Tell Him that you do believe that the Lord Jesus died for your sin and that He rose again. If you have told Him these things, and if you meant them with all your heart, the Lord Jesus did come in. Now, be sure to thank Him for dying for you.

CAIN AND ABEL

Scripture to be Studied: Genesis 4:1-15

Memory Verse:

He that believeth on Him is not condemned: but he that believeth not is condemned already, because he hath not believed in the name of the only begotten Son of God. (John 3:18)

Aim of the Lesson: To show that there is only one way of salvation and that is God's way, through the blood of the Lord Jesus Christ.

Show Illustration #24

"Mother, what was life like in the Garden of Eden?" Only one mother could answer that question. Eve must have heard her sons, Cain and Abel, ask the question more than once. "Life in the Garden of Eden was wonderful, boys. It was a beautiful place. God made it especially for your father and me, you know. There were no weeds. There was nothing to spoil the beauty. Every evening God Himself came and walked and talked with us."

"I wish we could have seen the Garden of Eden," Cain declared.

Eve sadly shook her head. "Never have we been able to go back into the garden–not since the day we disobeyed God. That was before you boys were born."

Adam, her husband, continued the explanation of their disobedience: "There were many beautiful plants and trees in the garden. There was plenty of food for us–delicious food. There was only one tree of which God said we were not to eat. We had plenty of food without that tree. Then one day Satan tempted us to eat that fruit. And we obeyed him. We did not want to meet God that evening. So we hid among the trees. But God found us. After He questioned us, we told Him all about our sin. Then God talked sternly to us."

"He told us," Eve added, "that we would have to leave the beautiful garden. He said that from then on weeds and thorns and thistles would grow. We would have to work hard to earn our living. There would be sickness and pain and sorrow."

The boys listened attentively. Very carefully Adam explained that which was most important of all. "God then killed an animal. He killed it, instead of killing us. Its coat of skin was made into coverings for our bodies. We deserved to die, because we had disobeyed God, the Holy One. But the animal died instead of us. God was satisfied with the blood of the animal as a covering for our sin. Ever since that day, whenever we bring an offering to the Lord, we bring an animal–the kind of animal which God has commanded. It is because of our sin that we can't come to God, except by shed blood. When God is satisfied with the blood of the animal which covers our sin, then we can talk to Him and worship Him. But this is the only way we can worship Him."

"It was after this," Eve reminded the boys, "that God put us out of the garden. He set angels at the garden gate. He put a flaming sword there, turning every direction, so we could never again enter the garden."

Each time their father offered the sacrifices for the family, Cain and Abel remembered what had happened to their parents. Adam built an altar for offering his sacrifice to God. He placed an animal (a lamb, doubtless) on the altar. (The Bible does not mention the altar. Nor does it say the offering was a lamb. But because of what the Bible says after this–about the offerings that were brought to God–we believe it must have been this way.) The throat of the lamb was cut and its blood poured out. Then the body of the lamb was burned on the altar as an offering to God. Together the family confessed their sins. The children of Adam and Eve were sinners, too, for they were born of parents who sinned. (Every person who has been born since that time has been born with the desire to sin.) God heard the prayers of Adam and his family and He forgave their sins. He gave them joy in worshiping Him.

Show Illustration #25

Cain and Abel never went to school. But they learned many things. Cain liked to dig and plant in the ground. When he grew up, he became a farmer–a good one. He was proud of the vegetables he grew. Abel liked animals and enjoyed tending sheep and lambs.

Then the time came when Cain and Abel were to bring sacrifices to the Lord. (Before that time, Adam had offered the sacrifices for the family. But when the boys were grown, it was no longer necessary for Adam to lead them in worship.)

Show Illustration #26

Abel built his altar. The wood for the burning of the sacrifice was laid in order on top of the altar. Abel was very careful in his selection of a lamb for his offering. It had to be a perfect lamb. And Abel made sure that he chose the best one.

Cain built his altar, too. But he did not select a lamb for his offering. It was strange that he did not do so, for he had never seen anything other than an animal offered. But Cain had a new idea. He would offer a different kind of sacrifice.

Cain forgot that the animal sacrifice was God's way. And that made a lot of difference! Cain looked at his fruits and vegetables–the things he himself had grown. They looked much nicer than a dead lamb. He could arrange his altar beautifully with fruits and vegetables on it. So this is exactly what he did. He chose the best, the nicest things he had raised. Of course there was no shed blood. But that did not matter to him. To Cain, his way was as good as Abel's way.

Cain looked toward Abel's altar. He could see the dead lamb. He could see that blood was shed.

The smoke of Abel's sacrifice was rising toward Heaven! Cain could see by the look of joy on Abel's face that God had let Abel know that He was satisfied with his offering. He knew, too, that God had forgiven Abel's sin. Then Cain looked toward his own sacrifice.

There was no sign of God's approval. Indeed, God did not accept his sacrifice. Cain knew God was not pleased. That made him angry. He scowled, showing the fury that was in his heart.

Then God spoke: "Cain, why are you angry? Why do you look so cross? You know that if you bring the right offering you will be accepted. You know I will forgive your sin if you obey Me. There is, even now, a lamb lying at your tent door. If you do not bring it, sin lies at the door of your heart."

But Cain turned from the Lord. Angrily he went away from the presence of God. Oh, how miserable was his heart! Ever since the day they had brought their offerings, Cain's hatred of Abel grew.

Not long afterward, Cain asked Abel to go out to the field together. And there Cain killed his brother Abel! The first person born into this world was a murderer!

Carefully Cain hid Abel's body.

Show Illustration #27

Then God called from Heaven, "Cain! Where is Abel your brother?" "I don't know," Cain lied. "Must I take care of my brother? He's not my responsibility."

"Cain, what have you done?" the Lord demanded. "I know that you killed your brother." Cain couldn't hide his sin. "Because you've done this," God added, "the ground will never again bring forth its best for you. Your crops will be small. The fruits and vegetables and grains will be of poor quality. You'll be a fugitive and tramp in the earth."

From that hour Cain wandered from place to place the rest of his life. Always he went on and on and on away from God.

(*Teacher:* If you are not using the *Pilgrim's Progress* story, you may want to give the following invitation here.)

Invitation

It is very important that we take God at His word. His word for us today is that we are to come to Him through His Son Who gave His life for us. Every time the blood of a lamb was shed in those years before the Lord Jesus died, God was looking forward to the day when the Lord Jesus would die to take away the sin of the world. That is why God was satisfied with the blood of the animals. Since then, however, the blood of the Lord Jesus–and the Lord Jesus alone-is the only sacrifice which God will accept. Only by believing in the Lord Jesus and receiving Him as Saviour from sin, can we be forgiven of our sins. If you have never received Him before, will you do so today?

Review Questions
by Hannah Pedrick

Chapter 1

1. Why did Paul decide to change his plans and go to Macedonia? *(He had a dream about a man from Macedonia asking him to come help them.)*

2. What did the girl from Macedonia do that was causing a problem for Paul and the other missionaries? *(She followed them everywhere they went, shouting.)*

3. What did Paul do to help this girl? *(He told the evil spirit to come out of her so she could be in her right mind again.)*

4. The men in charge of this girl were angry that she couldn't make money for them anymore, so what did they convince the city officials to do to Paul and Silas? *(Whip them and throw them into prison)*

5. What did Paul and Silas do as they were chained in that terrible prison? *(Sang songs of praise to God)*

6. What amazing thing suddenly happened as Paul and Silas were singing that night? *(There was an earthquake that broke the chains and opened the doors)*

7. When the jailor saw that Paul and the other prisoners had not run away, what did he decide to do? *(Believe in Jesus as the One Who could save him)*

8. What did the jailor do for Paul and Silas after he had decided to believe in Jesus? *(Took them to his home and took care of them)*

9. Discussion Question: The jailor asked Paul what he needed to do to be saved. What was Paul's answer? *(Believe on the Lord Jesus Christ)* Are there things we have to do to earn a way for our sins to be forgiven? *(Encourage the students to share their thoughts, but guide the discussion towards the finished work of Jesus.)*

10. Discussion Question: The first thing the jailor wanted to do after he had trusted in Jesus was make sure his family heard about Jesus, too. Do you know someone who needs to hear about Jesus? What are some ways you can tell them? *(Encourage the students to share their thoughts.)*

Chapter 2

1. What happened one night when Jesus took His disciples to a garden to pray? *(Soldiers came and arrested Jesus.)*

2. What did Jesus say when the high priest asked Him if He was the Son of God? *("I am!")*

3. Name some of the terrible things that Pilate's soldiers did to Jesus. *(Whipped Him, dressed Him in a purple robe, made fun of Him, put a crown of thorns on His head)*

4. Even though Pilate knew Jesus had done nothing wrong, what did he order his soldiers to do? (Crucify Jesus)

5. One of the thieves who was crucified with Jesus hated Him –how did the other thief feel about Jesus? *(He believed Jesus had not done anything wrong; asked Jesus to forgive him)*

6. What did Jesus' friends do with His body after He had died? *(Wrapped it in grave clothes and laid it in a tomb)*

7. When the women went to the tomb, what surprising things did they see? *(The stone was rolled away, the tomb was empty, an angel said Jesus was alive.)*

8. Later that day, what amazing thing happened as the disciples were alone in the locked room? *(Jesus appeared in the middle of the room and talked to them.)*

9. Discussion Question: Why didn't Jesus take Himself down off the cross? What does that kind of love mean to you? Do you think that knowing how much Jesus loves

you should change you in any way? (*Encourage the students to share their thoughts.*)

10. Discussion Question: What does it mean that Jesus is our Good Shepherd when we have believed in Him? What are some ways that Jesus is a Good Shepherd to you? (*Encourage the students to share their thoughts.*)

Chapter 3

1. As a Christian, what does the Bible say God gives us to protect ourselves in the battle against Satan? (*Armor*)

2. What does the Belt of Truth remind us to do in order to stay strong as a Christian? (*Always be truthful*)

3. What part of the Christian does the Breastplate of Righteousness protect? (*The heart*)

4. What are the Christian's shoes called? (*Good News of Peace shoes*)

5. When we put our faith in Jesus, whose attacks does the shield of faith protect us from? (*Satan*)

6. What does it mean for the Christian to wear the Helmet of Salvation? (*We are saved from our sins when we believe that Jesus died for us.*)

7. What is the Sword of the Spirit? (*The Bible, the Word of God*)

8. The armor from God is not things–it is a Person. Who is that Person? (*The Lord Jesus*)

9. Discussion Question: What are some of the ways that Satan tries to attack us? (*Encourage the students to share their thoughts.*)

10. Discussion Question: How can we be sure that we will win against Satan when we use the Armor of God? (*Encourage students to share their thoughts and guide the discussion toward remembering that Jesus is our armor, and He always wins the battle against sin and Satan.*)

Chapter 4

1. What big problem did the Hebrew people have at the beginning of our story? (They were slaves in Egypt)

2. What promise had God given to His people, the Hebrews? (Someday they would be set free and live in their own land)

3. After they were set free, how did God guide His people toward their new home? (By a cloud)

4. When his people complained, what did the Pharaoh of Egypt decide to do to the Hebrews? (Go with his army to bring them back as slaves)

5. What happened when Moses lifted his rod over the Red Sea, as God had told him to? (God sent a wind to make a dry pathway through the sea)

6. When the Hebrews began to cross the sea, why couldn't the Egyptians follow them right away? (Because God put

the cloud between them, and they could not see through the darkness)

7. When the Pharaoh and his army did begin to cross the Red Sea, what happened to them? (The walls of water fell on them)

8. How did the Hebrew people feel now that they were safe from the Egyptians? (*They praised God for taking care of them.*)

9. Discussion Question: Has there ever been a time when you prayed and asked God for help? Tell us about it. Can you share a way that God answered your prayer? (*Encourage students to share their thoughts.*)

10. Discussion Question: As God's people today, we have a worse enemy than Pharaoh. Who is this enemy? (*Satan*) Who can set us free from his power? (*Jesus*) How did Jesus do that? (*Encourage students to share their thoughts and guide the discussion toward Jesus' death and resurrection.*)

Chapter 5

1. What had Adam and Eve done that meant they could never return to the Garden of Eden? (*They disobeyed God and ate the fruit from the tree that He told them not to eat from.*)

2. What had God done to cover the sin of Adam and Eve? (*He killed an animal, whose blood was a covering for their sin.*)

3. What kind of jobs did Cain and Abel do when they grew up? (*Cain was a farmer and Abel took care of sheep.*)

4. Abel chose to sacrifice a perfect lamb, just as God had done –but what did Cain decide to give to God as a sacrifice instead? (*His best fruits and vegetables*)

5. Did God accept Cain's sacrifice? (*No*)

6. How did Cain feel when he saw that God had accepted Abel's sacrifice, but not his? (*He was very angry.*)

7. What terrible thing did Cain do to his brother? (*He killed him.*)

8. God knew what Cain had done. How did He punish Cain for murdering his brother? (*He could never grow good food again, and he'd have to wander the earth without a home.*)

9. Discussion Question: Why do you think God did not accept Cain's offering of fruits and vegetables? (*Encourage students to share their thoughts and guide the discussion toward the seriousness of sin and the need for a blood sacrifice.*)

10. Discussion Question: What do you think it was like in the Garden of Eden before Adam and Eve sinned? Can you imagine what life must have been like for Cain and Abel as the first children growing up on earth so many years ago? (*Encourage students to share their thoughts.*)

www.ingramcontent.com/pod-product-compliance
Lightning Source LLC
Chambersburg PA
CBHW042020080426
42735CB00002B/111